From Text to Knowledge A Comprehensive Guide to Natural Language Processing

David

TABLE OF CONTENTS

Chapter 1: Introduction to Natural Language Processing

What is Natural Language Processing?

Natural Language Processing (NLP) is a rapidly growing field that focuses on the interaction between computers and human language. It is a branch of artificial intelligence that enables machines to understand, interpret, and respond to human language in a meaningful way. NLP plays a crucial role in various applications, from virtual assistants and language translation to sentiment analysis and information extraction.

In simple terms, NLP is about teaching computers to understand and work with human language. It involves developing algorithms and models that allow machines to process and analyze textual data, just as humans do. By leveraging statistical and machine learning techniques, NLP algorithms can learn patterns, extract meaning, and generate coherent responses from text.

NLP encompasses several subtasks, including syntactic analysis, semantic analysis, named entity recognition, part-of-speech tagging, sentiment analysis, and machine translation, among others. These tasks collectively enable machines to understand the structure, meaning, and context of text, enabling them to extract valuable information and generate intelligent responses.

Data science and statistics are closely linked to NLP, as they provide the foundation for developing robust NLP models. NLP heavily relies on statistical methods for training and evaluating models, as well as for extracting meaningful insights from large volumes of textual data. Data scientists and statisticians play a vital role in developing and improving NLP techniques, by applying their expertise in data analysis, hypothesis testing, and experimental design.

For example, in sentiment analysis, data scientists employ statistical techniques to classify text as positive, negative, or neutral. They use labeled datasets to train machine learning models, which then learn to identify sentiment patterns in text data. Similarly, in machine translation, statisticians analyze large bilingual corpora to develop probabilistic models that accurately translate text from one language to another.

Understanding NLP is crucial in today's data-driven world, as it enables us to extract valuable insights from the vast amount of textual data available. Whether you are a data scientist, statistician, or simply someone interested in cutting-edge technology, learning about NLP will undoubtedly enhance your skills and open up new opportunities for analysis and automation.

In the following chapters, we will delve deeper into the various aspects of NLP, exploring different techniques, models, and applications. By the end of this book, you will have a comprehensive understanding of NLP and be equipped with the knowledge to apply it to real-world problems in data science and statistics.

History and Evolution of Natural Language Processing

Natural Language Processing (NLP) is a rapidly evolving field that has gained significant attention in recent years. It has revolutionized the way we interact with machines and has become an integral part of many applications we use daily, such as virtual assistants, chatbots, and language translation tools. This subchapter aims to provide a comprehensive overview of the history and evolution of NLP, from its humble beginnings to the advancements that have shaped it into what it is today.

The roots of NLP can be traced back to the 1950s, when researchers began exploring the possibilities of machine translation. The initial attempts were rule-based, relying on manually crafted linguistic rules, but they were limited in their ability to handle the complexity of language. In the 1960s, statistical approaches emerged, using probability models to determine the likelihood of word sequences. However, these methods also faced challenges due to the lack of computational power and data availability.

The 1980s marked a turning point with the introduction of machine learning techniques. Researchers started using large corpora of text to train models, which led to significant improvements in language processing tasks such as part-of-speech tagging and syntactic parsing. However, these models were still limited in their ability to understand the nuances of language and context.

The late 1990s and early 2000s saw the rise of statistical machine translation, driven by advancements in machine learning and the availability of vast amounts of parallel corpora. This approach, based on aligning sentences in different languages, paved the way for modern language translation systems.

The advent of deep learning in the 2010s revolutionized NLP. Deep neural networks, such as recurrent neural networks (RNNs) and transformers, brought breakthroughs in tasks like sentiment analysis, named entity recognition, and question-answering systems. The ability to process language at a more semantic level and capture contextual dependencies has led to significant improvements in NLP performance.

With the increasing availability of large-scale datasets, the emergence of pre-trained language models like BERT, GPT, and Transformer-XL has further pushed the boundaries of NLP. These models, trained on vast amounts of data, have achieved state-of-the-art results on various tasks and enabled transfer learning, allowing models to be fine-tuned for specific applications with smaller datasets.

As NLP continues to evolve, new challenges and opportunities arise. The integration of NLP with other domains, such as computer vision and knowledge graphs, has the potential to unlock even more powerful applications. The field is also exploring ways to address biases in language models and improve their interpretability.

In conclusion, the history and evolution of NLP have been marked by a series of milestones and breakthroughs, driven by advancements in technology, data availability, and computational power. As data scientists and statisticians, understanding this journey is crucial to grasp the current state of NLP and its potential for further advancements in the future.

Importance and Applications of Natural Language Processing

In today's digital era, the ability to process and understand human language is becoming increasingly crucial. Natural Language Processing (NLP) has emerged as a powerful field that focuses on the interaction between computers and human language. With its wide range of applications, NLP has gained immense importance in various domains, including data science and statistics.

NLP plays a vital role in extracting valuable insights from vast amounts of unstructured textual data. As the volume of text data continues to grow exponentially, NLP techniques enable data scientists and statisticians to efficiently analyze and make sense of this information. By leveraging NLP algorithms and models, they can uncover patterns, trends, and correlations hidden within text documents, providing valuable knowledge and actionable insights.

One of the key applications of NLP in data science and statistics is sentiment analysis. By employing NLP techniques, analysts can determine the sentiment or opinion expressed in text data, such as social media posts, customer reviews, or survey responses. This helps businesses understand customer satisfaction levels, identify emerging trends, and make informed decisions to improve products and services.

Another significant application of NLP is in information retrieval and search engines. NLP algorithms enable search engines to understand user queries and provide relevant search results based on the meaning and context of the query. This enhances the user experience by retrieving more accurate and tailored information, improving search engine rankings, and optimizing content discovery.

Furthermore, NLP is instrumental in text classification and categorization. By automatically assigning categories or labels to text documents, NLP algorithms make it easier to organize and filter large amounts of textual data. This is particularly helpful in areas such as spam detection, news categorization, and content recommendation systems.

NLP also plays a crucial role in machine translation, enabling computers to automatically translate text from one language to another. Machine translation systems utilize NLP techniques to analyze the structure and meaning of sentences, improving translation accuracy and fluency. This has significant implications for global communication, cross-cultural understanding, and business expansion.

In summary, NLP has become indispensable in the field of data science and statistics, offering valuable tools and techniques for extracting knowledge from text data. Its applications, including sentiment analysis, information retrieval, text classification, and machine translation, have revolutionized various industries and have the potential to drive innovation and decision-making. As more data is generated and the need for understanding human language grows, NLP will continue to play a pivotal role in transforming text into knowledge.

Chapter 2: Fundamentals of Text Mining

Introduction to Text Mining

Text mining, also known as text analytics, is a fascinating field within the realm of natural language processing (NLP). It involves the process of deriving meaningful insights and knowledge from unstructured textual data. In today's digital age, where vast amounts of text are generated every second, text mining has become a crucial tool for extracting valuable information from this data deluge.

This subchapter aims to provide a comprehensive introduction to text mining, catering to a wide audience, including data science and statistics enthusiasts. Whether you are a beginner or an expert in these fields, this chapter will equip you with the necessary knowledge to dive into the world of text mining and unlock the hidden potential of textual data.

Text mining encompasses a range of techniques, including information retrieval, natural language processing, machine learning, and statistical analysis. It involves the processing and analysis of text data in various forms, such as articles, social media posts, emails, customer reviews, and more. By applying computational methods to these texts, we can uncover patterns, relationships, and trends that contribute to a deeper understanding of the data.

In this subchapter, we will explore the key components of text mining, starting with the preprocessing steps necessary to transform raw text into a structured format suitable for analysis. We will cover techniques like tokenization, stop-word removal, stemming, and lemmatization, which aid in cleaning and organizing the text data.

Next, we will delve into the various approaches for representing text, such as bag-of-words, TF-IDF, and word embeddings. These methods allow us to convert textual data into numerical vectors, enabling the application of statistical and machine learning algorithms for further analysis.

We will also introduce different text mining tasks, including text classification, sentiment analysis, topic modeling, and named entity recognition. Each task serves a unique purpose, such as categorizing documents, identifying emotions, discovering latent themes, and extracting meaningful entities from text.

Furthermore, we will discuss the challenges and ethical considerations associated with text mining, including privacy concerns, biases, and the need for interpretability in machine learning models.

By the end of this subchapter, you will have a solid understanding of the fundamental concepts and techniques involved in text mining. Armed with this knowledge, you will be well-equipped to explore the vast possibilities of text mining in your own data science and statistical analyses, opening doors to valuable insights and knowledge hidden within the vast expanse of textual data.

So, let's embark on this exciting journey into the world of text mining together!

Text Preprocessing Techniques

Text preprocessing is a vital step in natural language processing (NLP) that helps transform raw text data into a format that can be easily understood and analyzed by machines. This subchapter explores various text preprocessing techniques that are commonly used in the field of NLP. Whether you are a data scientist or a statistician, understanding these techniques is essential for extracting valuable insights from textual data.

One of the first steps in text preprocessing is tokenization, where the text is divided into smaller units called tokens. These tokens can be words, phrases, or even individual characters depending on the task at hand. Tokenization is crucial as it serves as the foundation for subsequent analysis and feature extraction.

Stop word removal is another important technique in text preprocessing. Stop words are commonly used words in a language such as "and," "the," and "is." These words do not carry much meaning and can be safely removed to reduce the dimensionality of the data and improve processing efficiency.

Normalization is another essential preprocessing technique that aims to bring text data to a standard form. It involves converting all text to lowercase, removing punctuation marks, and handling special characters. Normalization ensures that variations in capitalization and formatting do not affect the analysis and modeling process.

Stemming and lemmatization are techniques used to reduce words to their base or root form. Stemming involves removing prefixes and suffixes from words, while lemmatization uses linguistic rules to convert words to their base form. These techniques help in reducing the vocabulary size and improving the accuracy of text analysis tasks such as sentiment analysis or topic modeling.

Handling special characters and encoding issues is also crucial in text preprocessing. Text data often contains special characters, emojis, or even multiple languages. It is important to handle these issues appropriately to avoid data corruption and ensure accurate analysis.

Finally, handling missing data and noise in text is crucial for robust analysis. Text data often contains missing values, typographical errors, or noisy elements. Dealing with these challenges involves techniques such as imputation, error correction, and noise reduction.

In conclusion, text preprocessing techniques are essential for transforming raw text data into a format suitable for analysis and modeling in NLP. Whether you are a data scientist or a statistician, understanding these techniques is crucial for extracting meaningful insights from textual data. Tokenization, stop word removal, normalization, stemming, lemmatization, handling special characters, and addressing missing data and noise are some of the key techniques discussed in this subchapter. By applying these techniques appropriately, you can unlock the full potential of text data and make informed decisions based on the knowledge extracted from it.

Text Representation and Feature Extraction

In the rapidly evolving field of Natural Language Processing (NLP), one of the key challenges is to transform unstructured text into a format that can be understood and processed by machines. This subchapter delves into the critical concepts of text representation and feature extraction, which are fundamental to extracting meaningful insights from textual data.

Text representation refers to the process of converting raw text into a numerical or symbolic form that can be effectively utilized by machine learning algorithms. This is essential because most statistical models and algorithms operate on numerical data. Various techniques have been developed to represent text, ranging from simple methods such as bag-of-words to more sophisticated approaches like word embeddings.

One of the most basic text representation techniques is the bag-of-words model. It treats each document as a collection of words and disregards the order or structure of the text. In this model, the frequency of occurrence of each word in a document is recorded, creating a vector representation of the text. While simple, this approach can provide valuable insights into text data.

However, the bag-of-words model ignores important aspects such as word context and semantic meaning. This limitation led to the development of word embeddings, which capture the semantic relationships between words. Word embeddings represent words as dense vectors in a high-dimensional space, where similar words are closer to each other. These embeddings are learned from large corpora of text using techniques like word2vec and GloVe.

Feature extraction is closely related to text representation and involves identifying relevant features or patterns in text data. These features are then used as inputs to machine learning algorithms. Feature extraction techniques can range from simple statistical measures such as word frequency and document length to more advanced techniques such as part-of-speech tagging and named entity recognition.

By leveraging text representation and feature extraction techniques, data scientists and statisticians can uncover valuable patterns and insights from textual data. Whether it is sentiment analysis, topic modeling, or text classification, these techniques form the foundation of many NLP applications. Understanding the strengths and limitations of different text representation and feature extraction methods is crucial for effectively analyzing and extracting knowledge from text data.

In summary, this subchapter provides an overview of the fundamental concepts of text representation and feature extraction in NLP. It explains how raw text is transformed into a format suitable for machine learning algorithms and highlights various techniques such as bag-of-words and word embeddings. By mastering these techniques, data scientists and statisticians can unlock the immense potential of textual data and gain deeper insights into the world of NLP.

Text Classification and Clustering

In the digital age, the amount of textual data available is growing exponentially, making it necessary to develop methods to extract valuable insights from this vast amount of information. Text classification and clustering are two fundamental techniques in natural language processing that enable us to organize, categorize, and analyze text data, providing us with a deeper understanding of the underlying patterns and structures.

Text classification involves categorizing text documents into predefined classes or categories. This technique is particularly useful when we have a large corpus of text data that needs to be organized and labeled. For instance, in email filtering, text classification can be used to automatically classify emails as spam or non-spam. Similarly, sentiment analysis, another application of text classification, helps us determine the sentiment expressed in a piece of text, such as positive, negative, or neutral.

On the other hand, text clustering is an unsupervised learning technique that groups similar documents together based on their content. Unlike text classification, which requires predefined categories, text clustering discovers the underlying structure in the data without any prior knowledge of the classes. This technique is valuable when we want to discover patterns or themes in a large collection of unclassified documents. For example, text clustering can be used to group news articles based on their topics or to identify similar documents in a legal case.

Both text classification and clustering techniques are essential tools for data scientists and statisticians. They enable us to transform unstructured textual data into structured information, making it easier to analyze and extract meaningful insights. These techniques have numerous applications across various industries, including marketing, customer service, healthcare, and finance.

In the field of data science, text classification and clustering techniques are frequently used to build predictive models, extract features, and perform exploratory analysis on large text datasets. By employing these techniques, data scientists can uncover hidden patterns, identify trends, and make data-driven decisions. In addition, statisticians can leverage text classification and clustering for hypothesis testing, data visualization, and modeling.

Understanding text classification and clustering is crucial for anyone working with textual data or interested in natural language processing. By mastering these techniques, individuals can unlock the potential of text data and gain valuable insights, contributing to advancements in various domains. Whether you are a data scientist, statistician, or simply curious about the power of language processing, this chapter will provide you with a comprehensive guide to text classification and clustering techniques, empowering you to extract knowledge from text and make informed decisions.

Chapter 3: Understanding Linguistics for Natural Language Processing

Introduction to Linguistics

Linguistics is the scientific study of language and its structure. It seeks to understand how language works, how it is used, and how it evolves over time. In this subchapter, we will delve into the fascinating world of linguistics and its relevance to the fields of data science and statistics.

Language is a fundamental aspect of human communication, enabling us to express our thoughts, ideas, and emotions. Whether spoken or written, language serves as the medium through which we exchange information and knowledge. Linguistics provides the tools and techniques to analyze and understand the intricacies of language, allowing us to gain insights into various aspects of human communication.

In the context of data science, linguistics plays a crucial role in natural language processing (NLP), a field that focuses on the interaction between computers and human language. NLP techniques enable machines to understand, interpret, and generate human language, facilitating tasks such as sentiment analysis, language translation, and information extraction. By applying linguistic principles and theories, data scientists can develop powerful algorithms and models to process and analyze vast amounts of textual data.

For statisticians, linguistics offers valuable insights into the statistical properties of language. Linguistic data can be analyzed using statistical methods to uncover patterns, trends, and relationships. By understanding the statistical properties of language, statisticians can develop models and algorithms that accurately capture and represent linguistic phenomena. This, in turn, enhances the accuracy and reliability of statistical analyses conducted on textual data.

In this subchapter, we will explore the key concepts and principles of linguistics, including phonetics (the study of speech sounds), phonology (the study of sound patterns), morphology (the study of word formation), syntax (the study of sentence structure), and semantics (the study of meaning). We will also examine the various applications of linguistics in NLP and statistical analysis.

Whether you are a data scientist, statistician, or simply someone interested in language and communication, this subchapter will provide you with a solid foundation in linguistics. By understanding the underlying principles of language, you will be better equipped to tackle the challenges and complexities of working with textual data, ultimately enhancing your ability to extract knowledge and insights from language.

Syntax and Semantics

In the realm of natural language processing, understanding the intricacies of syntax and semantics is paramount. These two fundamental aspects form the building blocks for comprehending the meaning and structure of human language. Whether you are a data scientist, statistician, or simply curious about the field, delving into the world of syntax and semantics will provide you with a deeper understanding of language processing.

Syntax refers to the rules and principles governing the arrangement of words to form grammatically correct sentences. It focuses on the structure and order of words, phrases, and clauses, enabling us to distinguish between well-formed and ill-formed sentences. A solid grasp of syntax is essential for developing robust language models and algorithms that can accurately parse and generate coherent sentences.

On the other hand, semantics deals with the meaning and interpretation of words, phrases, and sentences. It explores how words combine to convey specific meanings and how these meanings relate to the real world. Semantic analysis plays a crucial role in tasks such as sentiment analysis, information extraction, and question-answering systems. By understanding the semantics of language, we can unlock a deeper level of comprehension and extract valuable insights from textual data.

This subchapter will guide you through the intricacies of syntax and semantics, covering a range of topics such as grammatical structures, parsing techniques, semantic representation models, and word sense disambiguation. We will provide clear explanations, practical examples, and relevant applications to ensure that you grasp these concepts effectively.

For the data scientists and statisticians among you, understanding syntax and semantics can enhance your ability to work with large volumes of text data. By leveraging syntactic parsing techniques, you can extract valuable information from unstructured text and transform it into structured data suitable for analysis. Incorporating semantic analysis enables you to uncover deeper insights, identify patterns, and build predictive models that harness the power of language.

Regardless of your background or level of expertise, this subchapter will equip you with the necessary knowledge to navigate the world of syntax and semantics in natural language processing. By the end, you will have a solid foundation to further explore advanced techniques and applications in this exciting field. Let us embark on this journey to unravel the complexities of language and unlock the vast potential of natural language processing.

Morphology and Phonetics

Morphology and Phonetics: Understanding the Building Blocks of Language

Language is a wondrous human creation that allows us to express our thoughts, feelings, and ideas. But have you ever wondered how words are formed and how they are pronounced? Welcome to the fascinating world of morphology and phonetics, where we explore the building blocks of language.

Morphology is the study of how words are constructed and how they can be broken down into smaller units called morphemes. These morphemes are the smallest meaningful units of language, such as prefixes, suffixes, and root words. By understanding morphology, we can decipher the meaning of complex words and create new words by combining different morphemes. For example, in the word "unhappiness," we can identify the prefix "un-" meaning "not," the root word "happy," and the suffix "-ness" indicating a state or condition. Morphology provides us with the tools to analyze and manipulate words, making it an essential component of natural language processing.

Phonetics, on the other hand, deals with the sounds of language. It focuses on how sounds are produced, transmitted, and perceived. By studying phonetics, we can understand the physical properties of speech sounds and classify them into different categories. For instance, the sound "p" in "pat" is a voiceless bilabial stop, meaning it is produced by closing the lips and stopping the airflow without vocal cord vibration. Phonetics helps us transcribe and represent speech sounds accurately, which is crucial for tasks like speech recognition and synthesis.

The knowledge of morphology and phonetics is invaluable for data scientists and statisticians working with natural language processing. By understanding the structure and sounds of words, they can build more accurate models for tasks like sentiment analysis, machine translation, and information retrieval. For instance, by considering the morphological structure of words, we can identify relationships between different word forms and improve the performance of algorithms. Similarly, by accounting for phonetic variations, we can create more robust models that can handle different accents or dialects.

In conclusion, morphology and phonetics are essential for understanding the fundamental aspects of language. Whether you are a data scientist, statistician, or simply curious about how words are formed and pronounced, delving into these fields will unlock a deeper understanding of human communication. So, join us on this exciting journey as we unravel the mysteries of morphology and phonetics, and discover the incredible power of language processing.

Pragmatics and Discourse Analysis

Pragmatics and Discourse Analysis are two essential fields within Natural Language Processing (NLP) that play a significant role in understanding the complexities of human communication. In this subchapter, we will delve into these areas and explore their relevance to the broader field of NLP, with a particular focus on their applications in data science and statistics.

Pragmatics is concerned with the study of language in context. It investigates how people use language to convey meaning beyond the literal interpretation of words. Understanding pragmatics is crucial for NLP systems, as it helps in deciphering the intended meaning of a text, especially when dealing with ambiguous language or figurative expressions. Pragmatic analysis involves examining factors such as the speaker's intentions, the context of the communication, and the shared knowledge between the participants. By incorporating pragmatic knowledge into NLP models, we can enhance their ability to accurately interpret and generate human-like responses.

Discourse Analysis, on the other hand, focuses on the structure and organization of language beyond the sentence level. It examines how sentences are connected, how information is sequenced, and how meaning is constructed through the use of discourse markers, coherence relations, and other linguistic phenomena. Discourse analysis provides insights into how people create coherent and cohesive texts, allowing NLP systems to generate more coherent and contextually appropriate responses. Furthermore, it aids in tasks such as sentiment analysis, opinion mining, and information extraction by uncovering underlying patterns and relationships within a text.

In the realm of data science and statistics, pragmatics and discourse analysis have numerous practical applications. By incorporating pragmatic knowledge into natural language understanding models, data scientists can enhance the accuracy of sentiment analysis, enabling more nuanced interpretation of emotions expressed in text data. Moreover, discourse analysis techniques can be leveraged to identify patterns in large datasets, facilitating information extraction and knowledge discovery. These insights can be valuable in various domains, such as customer feedback analysis, market research, and social media monitoring.

In conclusion, pragmatics and discourse analysis are integral components of NLP that significantly contribute to the understanding and generation of human-like language. Their applications in data science and statistics can lead to more accurate sentiment analysis, efficient information extraction, and improved knowledge discovery. By incorporating these fields' principles into NLP models, we can enhance the performance and effectiveness of data-driven systems, ultimately advancing the field of natural language processing.

Chapter 4: Statistical Methods for Natural Language Processing

Introduction to Statistical Methods

Welcome to the subchapter on Introduction to Statistical Methods! In this section, we will explore the fundamental concepts and techniques that underpin the field of statistics and its relevance in data science. Whether you're a beginner or an experienced data scientist, this chapter will serve as a comprehensive guide to understanding statistical methods and their application in the world of natural language processing (NLP).

Statistics is the science of collecting, analyzing, interpreting, and presenting data. It provides us with the tools to make sense of complex data sets and draw meaningful insights from them. In the era of big data, statistical methods have become indispensable in various fields, including NLP, where they help us extract knowledge from vast amounts of textual data.

The primary goal of statistical methods is to make inferences and draw conclusions about a population based on a sample. Throughout this subchapter, we will explore various statistical techniques, such as hypothesis testing, regression analysis, and probability theory, that enable us to make reliable predictions and decisions from data.

Understanding statistical methods is crucial for anyone interested in data science and statistics. Whether you are a researcher, a business analyst, or simply curious about data analysis, statistical methods provide you with a powerful set of tools to uncover patterns, identify trends, and make informed decisions based on evidence.

In this subchapter, we will cover the basics of statistical methods, starting with the fundamental concepts such as variables, data types, and data distributions. We will then delve into descriptive statistics, which allow us to summarize and visualize data effectively. Next, we will explore probability theory, which forms the foundation of statistical inference and hypothesis testing.

Furthermore, we will discuss various statistical tests and techniques commonly used in NLP, including chi-square tests, t-tests, and ANOVA. We will also touch upon regression analysis and its application in NLP tasks like sentiment analysis and language modeling. Finally, we will explore the concept of statistical significance and its importance in drawing meaningful conclusions from data.

By the end of this subchapter, you will have a solid understanding of statistical methods and their application in NLP. Whether you plan to conduct research, build predictive models, or simply gain insights from textual data, the knowledge gained here will empower you to harness the power of statistics effectively.

So, let's embark on this statistical journey together and unlock the potential of data science and statistics in the realm of natural language processing!

Probability and Language Models

Probability and language models are fundamental concepts in the field of Natural Language Processing (NLP). Understanding these concepts is crucial for anyone interested in data science and statistics, as they form the basis for many NLP techniques and applications.

In the context of NLP, probability refers to the likelihood of a particular event or sequence of events occurring. It provides a quantitative measure of uncertainty and allows us to make informed decisions based on the likelihood of certain outcomes. In language modeling, probability is used to estimate the likelihood of a particular sequence of words occurring in a given language.

Language models, on the other hand, are statistical models that capture the patterns and structures of natural language. They are trained on large amounts of text data and learn the probabilities of word sequences. These models enable us to generate new text, evaluate the fluency of sentences, and even perform tasks such as machine translation and speech recognition.

One popular type of language model is the n-gram model, which predicts the probability of the next word in a sequence based on the previous n-1 words. For example, a trigram model would consider the two preceding words to predict the next word. N-gram models are simple yet effective in capturing local dependencies in language, but they struggle with long-range dependencies and suffer from the sparsity problem.

To address the limitations of n-gram models, more advanced models such as neural networks and recurrent neural networks (RNNs) have been developed. These models can capture long-range dependencies and have achieved state-of-the-art performance in various NLP tasks. They use probability distributions and mathematical functions to assign probabilities to different word sequences.

In NLP, probability and language models are used in a wide range of applications. They are essential for tasks like text classification, sentiment analysis, information retrieval, and machine translation. By understanding the underlying probability principles and language modeling techniques, data scientists and statisticians can design and develop more accurate and efficient NLP systems.

In conclusion, probability and language models are vital components of Natural Language Processing. They enable us to understand and quantify the uncertainty in language, and form the basis for many NLP techniques and applications. Whether you are a data scientist or a statistician, having a solid understanding of probability and language models will empower you to tackle complex NLP problems and contribute to the advancement of this exciting field.

Information Retrieval and Text Categorization

In today's digital age, we are constantly bombarded with vast amounts of information from various sources. With the exponential growth of online content, it has become increasingly challenging to find the information we need quickly and efficiently. This is where information retrieval and text categorization come into play.

Information retrieval is the process of finding and retrieving relevant information from a collection of documents or a database. It involves techniques and algorithms that enable us to search for specific documents or pieces of information based on user queries. Whether you are looking for a specific article, a book, or even a snippet of text, information retrieval systems strive to provide you with the most relevant and accurate results.

Text categorization, on the other hand, involves the classification of documents into predefined categories or topics. By analyzing the content of a document, text categorization algorithms can automatically assign it to the most appropriate category. This is particularly useful when dealing with large volumes of text, such as news articles or customer reviews, as it allows for efficient organization and retrieval of information.

Data science and statistics play a crucial role in the development and improvement of information retrieval and text categorization techniques. Through the analysis of large datasets, data scientists can identify patterns and trends that help optimize search algorithms and improve the accuracy of text categorization models. By leveraging statistical methods, they can also evaluate the performance of these systems and make informed decisions about their effectiveness.

For the general audience, understanding the basics of information retrieval and text categorization can greatly enhance their ability to navigate through the vast sea of information available today. By learning how to effectively search for information and categorize it, individuals can save valuable time and effort in their information-seeking endeavors.

For data scientists and statisticians, delving deeper into the intricacies of information retrieval and text categorization is essential. It enables them to develop more advanced algorithms, such as machine learning models, that can automatically learn and adapt to new data. These techniques are at the forefront of natural language processing and have numerous applications in fields such as information retrieval, sentiment analysis, and recommendation systems.

In conclusion, information retrieval and text categorization are crucial components of modern information processing. Whether you are a casual internet user or a data science enthusiast, understanding the fundamentals of these techniques can greatly enhance your ability to find and organize information effectively. By leveraging the power of data science and statistics, we can continue to improve these systems and unlock the full potential of natural language processing.

Sentiment Analysis and Opinion Mining

In today's digital age, where social media platforms, online forums, and review websites dominate our daily lives, understanding and analyzing public sentiment has become increasingly important. Sentiment analysis, also known as opinion mining, is a powerful technique that allows us to extract valuable insights from large volumes of text data. In this subchapter, we will delve into the world of sentiment analysis and explore its applications and methodologies.

Addressing a wide range of readers, from beginners to seasoned professionals, this subchapter aims to provide a comprehensive guide to sentiment analysis. Whether you are a data scientist looking to leverage sentiment analysis techniques or a statistician interested in understanding public opinion trends, this subchapter will equip you with the necessary knowledge to tackle real-world challenges.

Firstly, we will introduce the concept of sentiment analysis and its significance in various domains. We will discuss how sentiment analysis can be used to gauge public opinion on social media, analyze customer reviews, detect fake news, and even predict stock market trends. By understanding the underlying sentiments expressed in text data, individuals and organizations can make informed decisions and gain a competitive edge.

Next, we will explore the different methodologies and techniques employed in sentiment analysis. From rule-based approaches to machine learning algorithms, we will discuss their advantages, limitations, and implementation considerations. We will also delve into the challenges faced in sentiment analysis, such as sarcasm, irony, and cultural nuances, and present strategies to overcome them.

Furthermore, this subchapter will provide practical examples and case studies to illustrate the real-world applications of sentiment analysis. We will showcase how sentiment analysis has been used to monitor brand reputation, track public opinion during political campaigns, and identify emerging trends in consumer behavior. By examining these case studies, readers will gain a deeper understanding of how sentiment analysis can be effectively applied in their respective fields.

Finally, we will discuss the ethical implications of sentiment analysis and the importance of responsible data usage. We will address concerns regarding privacy, bias, and the potential misuse of sentiment analysis technology. By promoting transparency and ethical considerations, we aim to empower readers to leverage sentiment analysis responsibly.

In conclusion, this subchapter on sentiment analysis and opinion mining aims to cater to a diverse audience, including data scientists and statisticians. By providing a comprehensive guide to sentiment analysis techniques, methodologies, and applications, we hope to equip readers with the necessary tools to extract valuable insights from text data and make informed decisions in their respective domains.

Chapter 5: Neural Networks and Deep Learning in Natural Language Processing

Introduction to Neural Networks

Neural networks have revolutionized the field of data science and statistics, transforming the way we process and analyze complex information. In this subchapter, we will provide a comprehensive introduction to neural networks, shedding light on their fundamental concepts, working principles, and applications. Whether you are new to this field or an experienced data scientist, this chapter will serve as a valuable resource to enhance your understanding of neural networks.

Neural networks are computational models inspired by the structure and functioning of the human brain. Composed of interconnected nodes called artificial neurons or perceptrons, these networks excel at processing large amounts of data and extracting meaningful patterns. By mimicking the brain's ability to learn and adapt, neural networks have become a powerful tool in solving complex real-world problems.

We will begin by exploring the basic structure of neural networks. The building block of these networks is the artificial neuron, which receives input data, performs mathematical computations, and produces an output. These neurons are organized into layers, with each layer playing a unique role in the network's overall functioning. From the input layer to the output layer, information is processed and transformed through a series of interconnected neurons.

The next section delves into the concept of training neural networks. We will discuss the process of adjusting the weights and biases of the network's neurons to optimize its performance. This training phase involves feeding the network with known input-output pairs, allowing it to learn from example data and make accurate predictions on unseen data. We will also cover popular training algorithms and techniques, such as backpropagation, which enable neural networks to learn complex patterns and relationships.

Furthermore, we will explore various types of neural networks, including feedforward networks, recurrent networks, and convolutional networks. Each type is designed to handle specific tasks and exhibits unique characteristics. We will discuss their underlying architectures, applications, and advantages, providing you with a comprehensive understanding of when and how to employ them.

Lastly, we will examine the applications of neural networks in natural language processing. From sentiment analysis to machine translation, neural networks have revolutionized the way computers understand and generate human language. We will showcase some prominent examples, illustrating how neural networks have transformed the field and how you can leverage their power to extract knowledge from text data.

Whether you are a data scientist, statistician, or simply curious about neural networks, this subchapter will equip you with a solid foundation in understanding these powerful computational models. By the end, you will have gained a comprehensive overview of neural networks, enabling you to explore their applications and potential in your own data-driven projects.

Feedforward Neural Networks

Feedforward Neural Networks (FNNs) are a fundamental concept in the field of artificial intelligence and machine learning. In this subchapter, we will explore the inner workings of FNNs, their applications, and their significance in the field of natural language processing.

FNNs are a type of artificial neural network where the flow of information is unidirectional, moving from the input layer to the output layer without any feedback loops. This architecture allows FNNs to excel in tasks that require pattern recognition, classification, and regression analysis. By training on large datasets, FNNs can learn to recognize complex patterns and make accurate predictions or classifications based on the input data.

One of the key components of FNNs is the activation function. Activation functions introduce non-linearity into the network, enabling it to learn and represent complex relationships between inputs and outputs. Popular activation functions include the sigmoid, ReLU, and tanh functions, each with its own advantages and limitations.

FNNs have found widespread application in natural language processing tasks such as sentiment analysis, text classification, and language translation. By feeding textual data into the input layer, FNNs can learn to extract meaningful features and make predictions based on the learned patterns. This has revolutionized the way we process and understand textual information, enabling the development of intelligent chatbots, language translators, and text summarizers.

From a data science and statistical perspective, FNNs offer a powerful tool for analyzing and extracting insights from complex datasets. By leveraging their ability to recognize patterns and make predictions, FNNs can uncover hidden relationships and trends within the data. This has led to significant advancements in fields such as predictive analytics, customer segmentation, and anomaly detection.

Understanding the principles and applications of FNNs is crucial for anyone interested in the fields of data science and statistics. These networks provide a powerful and flexible framework for solving a wide range of real-world problems. By mastering FNNs, professionals in these niches can gain a competitive edge and contribute to the development of innovative solutions in their respective fields.

In conclusion, Feedforward Neural Networks are a fundamental concept in the field of artificial intelligence and machine learning. They offer a powerful tool for analyzing and processing textual data, enabling applications such as sentiment analysis and language translation. From a data science and statistical perspective, FNNs provide a flexible framework for uncovering patterns and making accurate predictions. By understanding the inner workings and applications of FNNs, professionals in the fields of data science and statistics can unlock valuable insights and contribute to the advancement of their respective disciplines.

Recurrent Neural Networks

Recurrent Neural Networks (RNNs) are a class of artificial neural networks that have gained significant popularity in the field of natural language processing (NLP) due to their ability to process sequential data. In this subchapter, we will explore the fundamentals of RNNs and how they are applied in NLP tasks, making it an essential read for anyone interested in data science and statistics.

RNNs are unique compared to other neural networks because they can retain information from previous inputs, making them ideal for tasks involving sequential data. This characteristic enables RNNs to capture the context and dependencies among words in a sentence or the order of events in a time series. By modeling the temporal aspects of the data, RNNs have shown impressive results in various NLP tasks such as language modeling, machine translation, sentiment analysis, and named entity recognition.

To comprehend RNNs, it is crucial to understand their architecture. At its core, an RNN consists of recurrent units connected in a chain-like structure. Each unit takes an input, processes it, and passes the output to the next unit while maintaining an internal state. This internal state acts as a memory that captures the information from past inputs and influences the processing of future inputs. This memory concept enables RNNs to capture long-term dependencies and effectively handle variable-length sequences.

One of the most widely used RNN variants is the Long Short-Term Memory (LSTM) network. LSTMs address the vanishing gradient problem, a common issue in training deep neural networks, by introducing specialized memory cells that selectively retain or forget information. This modification allows LSTMs to process longer sequences and capture more complex dependencies.

Furthermore, RNNs can be stacked to create deep recurrent networks, enhancing their representational power and ability to model intricate relationships in the data. Deep RNNs have proven highly effective in tasks such as speech recognition, where the input data comprises a stream of acoustic features.

In summary, recurrent neural networks have revolutionized the field of natural language processing by enabling the modeling of sequential data. Their ability to capture temporal dependencies and retain information from previous inputs makes them a powerful tool for various NLP tasks. Whether you are a data scientist, statistician, or simply interested in understanding the applications of neural networks in language processing, this subchapter will provide you with a comprehensive understanding of recurrent neural networks and their significance in the field.

Convolutional Neural Networks

Convolutional Neural Networks (CNNs) have revolutionized the field of artificial intelligence, particularly in the domain of computer vision. In this subchapter, we will explore the fundamentals of CNNs and delve into their applications in natural language processing (NLP). This knowledge is essential for anyone interested in data science and statistics.

CNNs are a type of deep learning model inspired by the visual cortex of the human brain. They are designed to automatically learn and extract features from input data, making them highly effective in analyzing complex patterns and structures. Originally developed for image recognition tasks, CNNs have since been successfully adapted for NLP tasks, such as text classification, sentiment analysis, and machine translation.

The key component of a CNN is the convolutional layer. This layer applies a set of filters or kernels to the input data, which helps to capture local patterns and spatial relationships. Through the process of convolution, these filters slide across the input, computing dot products at each position and producing feature maps. This allows the network to learn hierarchical representations of the input, starting with low-level features (e.g., edges, corners) and progressively extracting higher-level features (e.g., shapes, objects).

In addition to convolutional layers, CNNs also incorporate pooling layers, which reduce the dimensionality of the learned features while preserving their important characteristics. Pooling helps to make the network more robust to slight variations in the input and improves computational efficiency.

To make CNNs suitable for NLP tasks, the input data needs to be transformed into a format that can be processed by the network. This typically involves representing words as vectors, either using pre-trained word embeddings or by training them from scratch on a large corpus. These word vectors are then fed into the CNN, which learns to recognize relevant patterns and relationships between words.

By leveraging the power of CNNs, researchers and practitioners in the field of NLP have achieved remarkable results on a wide range of tasks. CNN-based models have significantly improved the accuracy of sentiment analysis, text classification, and even machine translation. These models have also paved the way for more advanced architectures, such as attention-based models and transformer networks.

In conclusion, Convolutional Neural Networks are a powerful tool in the realm of natural language processing. Their ability to automatically learn and extract meaningful features from input data has revolutionized the field, enabling breakthroughs in various NLP tasks. Whether you are a data scientist or statistician, understanding the fundamentals of CNNs is crucial for staying at the forefront of NLP research and application.

Applications of Deep Learning in Natural Language Processing

Deep learning, a subfield of machine learning, has revolutionized the field of natural language processing (NLP) by enabling computers to understand and generate human language. This subchapter will explore the various applications of deep learning in NLP, highlighting its significance in advancing the field and its potential to benefit a wide range of industries and domains.

One of the most prominent applications of deep learning in NLP is in language translation. Deep learning models, such as neural machine translation (NMT) systems, have shown remarkable performance in translating text from one language to another. These models learn to map sentences from the source language to the target language, capturing complex linguistic patterns and nuances. NMT systems have significantly improved the accuracy and fluency of machine translation, making it invaluable for global communication and breaking language barriers.

Another application lies in sentiment analysis and opinion mining. Deep learning models can automatically classify text based on sentiment, allowing businesses to analyze customer feedback, social media posts, and reviews at scale. By understanding customer sentiment, companies can make data-driven decisions, enhance customer experience, and improve their products or services.

Deep learning also plays a crucial role in text generation tasks, like speech synthesis and chatbot development. These applications rely on recurrent neural networks (RNNs) or transformer models to generate coherent and contextually relevant responses. Speech synthesis is useful for applications such as virtual assistants and audiobook narration, while chatbots enable human-like interactions and customer support.

Furthermore, deep learning models have been successful in text summarization and information extraction tasks. By leveraging techniques like attention mechanisms and transformer models, these models can generate concise summaries from lengthy documents or extract relevant information from unstructured text. Such capabilities find applications in news aggregation, document summarization, and knowledge extraction from large corpora.

In addition to these applications, deep learning has also proven effective in natural language understanding tasks, including named entity recognition, sentiment analysis, question answering, and document classification. These advancements have paved the way for intelligent search engines, automated content categorization, and recommendation systems.

Overall, deep learning has brought significant advancements to NLP, enabling machines to understand, generate, and process human language more effectively. Its applications extend across various domains, including e-commerce, healthcare, finance, and marketing. As the field of NLP continues to evolve, deep learning will undoubtedly play a vital role in unlocking the full potential of natural language understanding and communication.

Chapter 6: Word Embeddings and Language Models

Introduction to Word Embeddings

Word embeddings have revolutionized the field of natural language processing (NLP) and have become an integral part of various applications in data science and statistics. In this subchapter, we will provide an introduction to word embeddings, explaining what they are and how they can be used to enhance our understanding of textual data.

At its core, word embedding is a technique used to represent words in a continuous vector space, where words with similar meanings are located closer to each other. This approach captures the semantic relationships between words, allowing machines to understand the contextual meaning of words in a given text. Instead of treating words as discrete units, word embeddings enable us to analyze the meaning of words based on their distributional properties within a large corpus of text.

One of the popular methods for generating word embeddings is called Word2Vec, which employs a neural network architecture to learn word representations from large datasets. The Word2Vec model is trained on a large corpus of text and learns to predict the probability of a word occurring in its context. Through this process, it creates dense vector representations for each word, capturing both syntactic and semantic information.

Word embeddings have numerous applications in data science and statistics. They can be used to improve the performance of various NLP tasks, such as sentiment analysis, named entity recognition, machine translation, and text classification. By utilizing word embeddings, these tasks can leverage the semantic relationships between words, leading to more accurate results.

Furthermore, word embeddings enable us to perform calculations with words. For example, we can add or subtract word vectors to find analogies or similarities between words. For instance, by subtracting the vector representation of "king" from "man" and adding the vector representation of "woman," we obtain a vector close to "queen." This ability to perform vector arithmetic with words opens up possibilities for applications like word analogies and recommendation systems.

In this subchapter, we will delve deeper into the mechanics of word embeddings and explore different techniques for training word embeddings. We will also discuss the evaluation metrics used to assess the quality of word embeddings. By the end of this subchapter, you will have a solid understanding of word embeddings and their relevance to data science and statistics, empowering you to leverage their power in various NLP applications.

Word2Vec and GloVe Models

In the realm of natural language processing (NLP), Word2Vec and GloVe models have revolutionized the way we understand and process text data. These models have become powerful tools for data scientists and statisticians to extract meaningful insights from vast amounts of textual information.

Word2Vec, short for Word to Vector, is an algorithm that learns word embeddings from large corpora. It maps words to high-dimensional vectors, capturing their semantic and syntactic relationships. By representing words as continuous vector spaces, Word2Vec enables machines to understand the meaning of words based on their context in a given text. This technique has proven to be highly effective in various NLP tasks, including language modeling, named entity recognition, sentiment analysis, and machine translation.

GloVe, or Global Vectors for Word Representation, is another popular word embedding model. It utilizes co-occurrence statistics of words to create word vectors. Unlike Word2Vec, which focuses on local context, GloVe considers the global word co-occurrence frequencies across the entire corpus. This approach allows GloVe to capture both semantic and syntactic information, making it a valuable tool for NLP tasks such as word analogy, word similarity, and text classification.

Both Word2Vec and GloVe models have their strengths and can be applied to various domains. They excel in capturing word semantics and offer numerical representations that facilitate mathematical operations on words. This makes them particularly useful in downstream machine learning tasks where textual data needs to be transformed into a numerical format for further analysis.

Data scientists and statisticians can leverage the power of Word2Vec and GloVe models to gain deeper insights from text data. These models can help identify important patterns, extract contextual information, and improve the accuracy of predictive models. With the ability to understand the meaning of words in a given context, these models enable sophisticated analysis and interpretation of textual information.

It is worth noting that Word2Vec and GloVe models are not limited to English language texts. They can be trained on corpora from any language, enabling multilingual applications of NLP techniques. By bridging the gap between human language and machine understanding, these models open up a world of possibilities for data scientists and statisticians working with textual data.

In conclusion, Word2Vec and GloVe models are powerful tools in the field of NLP. They offer a means to extract knowledge and insights from text data, making them invaluable for data scientists and statisticians. By utilizing these models, professionals in the field can unlock the potential of textual information and enhance their data-driven decision-making processes.

Contextual Word Embeddings (BERT, ELMO)

In recent years, the field of Natural Language Processing (NLP) has witnessed significant advancements, particularly in the area of word embeddings. Word embeddings play a crucial role in understanding the meaning of words and their relationships within a given text. Traditional word embeddings, such as Word2Vec and GloVe, have been widely used, but they often fail to capture the contextual information of words.

To overcome this limitation, a new breed of word embeddings has emerged: contextual word embeddings. Two popular models in this category are BERT (Bidirectional Encoder Representations from Transformers) and ELMO (Embeddings from Language Models). These models have revolutionized NLP by providing a deeper understanding of language semantics and syntax.

BERT, developed by Google, is a pre-trained language model that uses transformer architecture. It is trained on a massive corpus of text, enabling it to learn the context and meaning of words. BERT's key innovation lies in its bidirectional approach, where it considers both left and right context while generating word embeddings. This enables BERT to capture complex relationships between words, resulting in more accurate representations.

ELMO, on the other hand, introduced by researchers at Allen Institute for Artificial Intelligence, also utilizes a deep bidirectional language model. ELMO leverages the idea that word meanings can change depending on the context. Instead of generating a single static embedding for a word, ELMO computes contextual embeddings by considering the entire sentence. This approach allows ELMO to capture fine-grained nuances in language and produce highly context-dependent word representations.

Both BERT and ELMO have been widely adopted in various NLP tasks, including sentiment analysis, named entity recognition, and question-answering systems. Their ability to generate rich, contextualized word embeddings has significantly improved the performance of these tasks, pushing the boundaries of what was previously possible in NLP.

For data scientists and statisticians, understanding and utilizing contextual word embeddings can greatly enhance their NLP models' accuracy and effectiveness. By incorporating BERT or ELMO into their workflows, they can extract more meaningful information from textual data, leading to better insights and predictions.

In conclusion, contextual word embeddings, such as BERT and ELMO, have brought a new level of sophistication to NLP. Their ability to capture context and generate highly contextualized word representations has revolutionized the field. For anyone interested in data science and statistics, these models offer a powerful tool to unlock the knowledge hidden within text and push the boundaries of what can be achieved in natural language processing.

Language Models and Transfer Learning

In recent years, language models and transfer learning have emerged as game-changers in the field of natural language processing (NLP). These techniques have revolutionized the way we build and train models, enabling us to extract knowledge from text more effectively than ever before. This subchapter explores the concepts of language models and transfer learning, shedding light on their significance and applications in various domains, particularly for data science and statistics enthusiasts.

Language models, at their core, are statistical models that learn the patterns and relationships between words in a given language. They capture the semantics, grammar, and context of sentences, allowing machines to understand human language. Traditional language models, such as n-gram models, have limitations due to their inability to capture long-range dependencies and context. However, recent advancements in deep learning have given rise to highly sophisticated language models like transformer-based architectures, such as BERT (Bidirectional Encoder Representations from Transformers), GPT (Generative Pre-trained Transformer), and XLNet, which have overcome many of these limitations.

Transfer learning, on the other hand, leverages pre-trained models to tackle new tasks. Instead of training models from scratch, transfer learning involves using existing knowledge from pre-trained models, fine-tuning them on specific tasks, and transferring this learned knowledge to new domains. This approach significantly reduces the computational resources and labeled data required for training, making it highly efficient and practical.

The combination of language models and transfer learning has led to remarkable advancements in NLP. By pre-training on vast amounts of unlabeled text data, language models like BERT and GPT have learned to understand the nuances of language, resulting in state-of-the-art performance on a wide range of NLP tasks. These models have been trained on diverse texts, including books, websites, and articles, and have acquired a deep understanding of language semantics, enabling them to generate coherent and contextually relevant responses.

For data science and statistics enthusiasts, language models and transfer learning offer endless possibilities. They can be used to extract insights from large text datasets, perform sentiment analysis, automate customer support, generate human-like text, and even assist in machine translation. These techniques allow data scientists to leverage the power of language to gain new knowledge from text, enabling them to make informed decisions and drive innovation.

In conclusion, language models and transfer learning have revolutionized the field of NLP, unlocking new possibilities for data science and statistics enthusiasts. These techniques have empowered machines to understand human language better than ever before, enabling them to extract knowledge from text and perform a wide range of tasks. By leveraging pre-trained models and transferring learned knowledge, data scientists can now leverage the power of language to gain valuable insights and drive innovation in various domains. The future of NLP is undoubtedly bright, with language models and transfer learning at the forefront of this transformative journey.

Chapter 7: Information Extraction and Named Entity Recognition

Introduction to Information Extraction

In today's digital age, the amount of information available to us is simply overwhelming. From news articles and social media posts to scientific papers and business reports, the sheer volume of textual data is staggering. But how can we make sense of all this information? How can we extract valuable insights and knowledge from these vast amounts of text?

This subchapter, "Introduction to Information Extraction," aims to provide a comprehensive introduction to the field of Natural Language Processing (NLP) and its applications in data science and statistics. Whether you are a beginner in the field or an experienced data scientist, this chapter will equip you with the necessary tools and techniques to extract meaningful information from unstructured text.

Information extraction is a crucial component of NLP that focuses on identifying and extracting structured information from unstructured text. It involves techniques such as named entity recognition, part-of-speech tagging, and relation extraction, among others. By employing these techniques, we can transform unstructured text into structured data that can be analyzed and used for various purposes.

This subchapter begins by providing an overview of the fundamental concepts and techniques in information extraction. We will explore the different types of information that can be extracted, including entities, relationships, and events. Furthermore, we will delve into the challenges and complexities associated with information extraction, such as ambiguity, context, and domain-specific knowledge.

Next, we will discuss the various methods and algorithms used in information extraction. We will explore both rule-based approaches and machine learning techniques, highlighting their strengths and limitations. Additionally, we will delve into the importance of feature engineering and the role of domain knowledge in improving extraction accuracy.

To illustrate the practical applications of information extraction, we will explore real-world use cases in data science and statistics. We will showcase how information extraction can be used to analyze social media data, extract insights from scientific literature, and automate data entry and extraction tasks. By understanding these applications, you will gain a deeper appreciation for the power of information extraction in uncovering hidden patterns and knowledge from text.

In conclusion, "Introduction to Information Extraction" is a comprehensive guide that will equip you with the knowledge and techniques necessary to extract valuable information from unstructured text. Whether you are a data scientist, statistician, or simply someone interested in the field, this subchapter will empower you to make the most of the vast amount of textual data available today. So, let's embark on this exciting journey into the world of information extraction and unlock the true potential of text to knowledge.

Named Entity Recognition Techniques

Named Entity Recognition (NER) is a crucial task in Natural Language Processing (NLP) that involves identifying and classifying named entities in text. Named entities refer to specific words or phrases that represent real-world objects such as people, organizations, locations, dates, and more. NER plays a vital role in various NLP applications, including information extraction, question answering, machine translation, and sentiment analysis.

This subchapter introduces the different techniques employed for Named Entity Recognition, providing a comprehensive overview of the methods used to tackle this challenging task. By understanding these techniques, you will be able to extract meaningful information from unstructured text data and gain valuable insights.

1. Rule-based Approaches: Rule-based approaches rely on pre-defined patterns and handcrafted rules to identify named entities. These rules can be based on regular expressions, dictionaries, or grammatical structures. While rule-based systems can be effective in certain domains, they often require domain-specific knowledge and manual effort to create and maintain the rules.

2. Machine Learning Approaches: Machine Learning (ML) techniques have revolutionized NER by enabling automated entity recognition. ML models are trained on annotated datasets, where human annotators label text with named entities. These models then learn to identify entities based on various features, such as word context, part-of-speech tags, and syntactic information. Popular ML algorithms for NER include Conditional Random Fields (CRF), Hidden Markov Models (HMM), and deep

learning models like Recurrent Neural Networks (RNN) and Transformer-based architectures.

3.   Hybrid   Approaches: Hybrid approaches combine the strengths of both rule-based and machine learning techniques. They incorporate handcrafted rules as well as ML models to improve entity recognition accuracy. These approaches leverage ML models to automatically learn patterns and rules from annotated data, enhancing the performance and flexibility of the system.

4.   Deep   Learning   Approaches: Deep Learning techniques have gained significant attention in NER due to their ability to capture intricate patterns and relationships within text data. Deep Learning models, such as Long Short-Term Memory (LSTM) networks and Transformer-based architectures (e.g., BERT), have achieved state-of-the-art performance on various NER benchmarks. These models can capture contextual information effectively and generalize well to different domains.

Understanding the different Named Entity Recognition techniques is essential for data scientists and statisticians working with NLP tasks. It enables them to choose the most suitable approach based on their specific requirements and data characteristics. By leveraging these techniques, you can extract valuable information from text data, facilitating knowledge discovery and decision-making processes.

Relation Extraction and Event Extraction

In the world of natural language processing, Relation Extraction and Event Extraction are two fundamental tasks that play a crucial role in transforming unstructured text into structured knowledge. These tasks enable us to unlock hidden relationships and events within textual data, thereby facilitating more advanced analysis and understanding.

Relation Extraction involves the identification and extraction of relationships between entities mentioned in a text. Entities can refer to people, organizations, locations, or any other named entities of interest. By determining the relationships between these entities, we can gain valuable insights into the connections and interactions within a given corpus. For example, relation extraction can help us uncover connections between people and their affiliations, such as identifying the CEO of a company or the author of a book.

Event Extraction, on the other hand, focuses on identifying and extracting events or occurrences mentioned in a text. Events can include anything from natural disasters and political elections to sports matches and scientific experiments. By extracting these events, we can build event databases that enable us to analyze patterns, trends, and correlations. For instance, event extraction can help us track disease outbreaks, monitor stock market fluctuations, or analyze social media sentiment during a specific event.

Both Relation Extraction and Event Extraction rely on various techniques and approaches, including rule-based methods, machine learning algorithms, and deep learning models. These methods leverage linguistic patterns, syntactic structures, and semantic information to identify relevant entities, relationships, and events within text. They often require large annotated datasets for training and may involve domain-specific knowledge to improve accuracy and performance.

The applications of Relation Extraction and Event Extraction are vast and diverse, making them essential tools for data scientists and statisticians. These tasks are particularly valuable in fields like social network analysis, information retrieval, knowledge graph construction, and sentiment analysis. By extracting and linking relationships and events from textual data, these professionals can gain a deeper understanding of trends, patterns, and causality, ultimately leading to more informed decision-making.

In conclusion, Relation Extraction and Event Extraction are vital components of natural language processing, enabling the transformation of unstructured text into structured knowledge. These tasks offer valuable insights into the relationships between entities and the occurrences of events, facilitating advanced analysis and understanding. By leveraging various techniques and approaches, data scientists and statisticians can unlock the power of textual data and drive meaningful insights across a wide range of domains.

Coreference Resolution

Coreference resolution is a fundamental task in natural language processing (NLP) that aims to identify expressions in a text that refer to the same entity or concept. It plays a crucial role in understanding the relationships between various elements in a sentence or a document. Whether you are a data scientist or a statistician, having a solid understanding of coreference resolution is essential for extracting meaningful insights from text data.

In simple terms, coreference resolution helps us determine the antecedent or the referent of a pronoun or a noun phrase. For example, consider the sentence: "John went to the store. He bought some groceries." Here, the pronoun "he" refers back to the noun phrase "John." Coreference resolution algorithms are designed to automatically recognize such relationships and establish the correct references.

Why is coreference resolution important? Well, imagine you are analyzing a large corpus of documents, and you come across a sentence like: "Apple announced a new product today. It is the most innovative device yet." Without coreference resolution, you might not be able to link the pronoun "it" to the noun phrase "new product." Consequently, your analysis could be incomplete or inaccurate.

To achieve accurate coreference resolution, NLP researchers have developed various approaches. These approaches can be broadly categorized into rule-based, statistical, and machine learning-based methods. Rule-based methods rely on linguistic rules and patterns to identify coreferent expressions. Statistical approaches, on the other hand, utilize probabilistic models to capture the likelihood of coreference between different expressions. Machine learning-based methods leverage annotated datasets to train models that can predict coreference relations.

While coreference resolution algorithms have significantly advanced in recent years, challenges still remain. Resolving coreference accurately in complex sentences, dealing with ambiguous references, and handling entity types and mentions are some of the ongoing research areas.

In conclusion, coreference resolution is a vital component of natural language processing, enabling computers to understand the relationships between different elements in a text. As a data scientist or a statistician, having knowledge of coreference resolution allows you to unlock valuable insights from text data and build more sophisticated NLP models. Whether you are working on sentiment analysis, information extraction, or question answering, a solid understanding of coreference resolution will undoubtedly enhance your capabilities in the field of data science and statistics.

Chapter 8: Machine Translation and Language Generation

Introduction to Machine Translation

Machine translation is a fascinating field within the realm of natural language processing that has gained significant importance in recent years. With the increasing availability of large amounts of multilingual data and advances in computing power, machine translation has become a powerful tool for breaking down language barriers and enabling communication across different cultures and countries.

This subchapter serves as an introduction to machine translation, providing an overview of the fundamental concepts and techniques used in this field. Whether you are a data scientist, statistician, or simply someone interested in understanding the inner workings of machine translation, this chapter will provide you with a solid foundation.

We will begin by exploring the history of machine translation, tracing its origins back to the early days of computing. From rule-based systems to statistical approaches and the recent rise of neural machine translation, we will discuss the evolution of machine translation techniques and their impact on the quality of translations.

Next, we will delve into the key components of a machine translation system. You will learn about the importance of parallel corpora, which are collections of texts in multiple languages that serve as training data for machine translation models. We will also examine the different steps involved in the machine translation process, including pre-processing, alignment, and decoding.

Furthermore, we will explore the various approaches to machine translation, such as rule-based, statistical, and neural machine translation. We will discuss the strengths and limitations of each approach and how they have contributed to the advancements in machine translation over time.

Additionally, we will cover evaluation metrics used to assess the quality of machine translation systems. You will gain insights into how human evaluations are conducted and the challenges involved in measuring the accuracy and fluency of translations.

Finally, we will touch upon some of the current applications of machine translation, including its role in aiding human translators, enabling cross-cultural communication on social media platforms, and facilitating multilingual information retrieval.

By the end of this subchapter, you will have a solid understanding of the fundamental concepts, techniques, and applications of machine translation. Whether you are interested in pursuing a career in data science, statistics, or simply want to explore the exciting world of natural language processing, this subchapter will serve as a valuable resource to get you started on your journey.

Rule-Based Machine Translation

In the rapidly evolving field of Natural Language Processing (NLP), one of the key challenges is to enable computers to understand and translate human languages with accuracy and efficiency. Machine translation, in particular, holds immense potential for breaking down language barriers and facilitating global communication. Among various approaches to machine translation, rule-based machine translation (RBMT) has garnered significant attention. In this subchapter, we will delve into the concept of RBMT and its relevance in the field of NLP.

Rule-based machine translation, as the name suggests, relies on a set of linguistic rules to translate text from one language to another. These rules are created by linguists and language experts who analyze the grammatical structures, syntax, and semantics of both the source and target languages. The key advantage of RBMT is its ability to capture the nuances and intricacies of language, making it suitable for translating complex texts such as legal documents, technical manuals, and medical literature.

RBMT operates on the basis of a rule engine, which consists of a series of if-then statements that guide the translation process. These rules encompass grammatical rules, lexical rules, syntactic rules, and semantic rules, among others. For instance, if a rule engine encounters a specific grammatical structure in the source language, it will apply the corresponding rule to generate the appropriate translation in the target language.

While rule-based machine translation offers the advantage of linguistic accuracy, it also has certain limitations. One of the major challenges is the labor-intensive process of rule creation, which requires extensive linguistic expertise and manual effort. Additionally, RBMT struggles with translating idiomatic expressions, colloquialisms, and languages with complex word order. The rigid nature of rule-based systems also makes it difficult to adapt to changes and updates in languages, resulting in the need for constant maintenance and updates.

However, RBMT still plays a crucial role in specific domains, particularly in fields such as legal translation, where accuracy and precision are paramount. Moreover, RBMT can be combined with other machine translation approaches, such as statistical machine translation and neural machine translation, to leverage their respective strengths.

In conclusion, rule-based machine translation is a linguistic-driven approach that utilizes a set of predefined rules to translate text from one language to another. While it has its limitations, RBMT remains an important tool in certain domains, offering accurate and precise translations. As the field of NLP continues to advance, RBMT provides valuable insights and serves as a foundation for developing more advanced machine translation systems.

Statistical and Neural Machine Translation

Translation of languages has always been a fascinating yet challenging task for humans. With the advent of computers and the progress in natural language processing, machine translation has become increasingly important. In this subchapter, we will delve into the two prominent approaches to machine translation: statistical and neural machine translation.

Statistical machine translation (SMT) is a method that relies on statistical models to learn patterns and relationships between words and phrases in different languages. It operates by aligning parallel texts, such as a source sentence in one language and its translation in another language, to establish patterns. SMT models use statistical algorithms to estimate the probability of a particular translation given a source sentence. This approach has been widely used for a considerable time, and it paved the way for the development of more advanced translation systems.

However, the recent breakthrough in deep learning and artificial neural networks has led to the emergence of neural machine translation (NMT). Unlike SMT, NMT utilizes neural networks to learn the mapping between a source sentence and its translation. This approach has shown remarkable improvements in translation quality, thanks to its ability to capture complex linguistic patterns and context.

Both statistical and neural machine translation have their strengths and weaknesses. SMT, with its reliance on statistical models, has proven to be effective when there is limited parallel data available for training. It is also more interpretable, allowing researchers to analyze and understand the underlying patterns in translation. On the other hand, NMT has shown superior performance in terms of translation accuracy and fluency. Its ability to model complex linguistic phenomena, such as word order and context, has made it the preferred choice for many translation tasks.

For data scientists and statisticians, understanding the intricacies of statistical and neural machine translation can open up numerous opportunities. These approaches are not only limited to translating text but can also be applied to various language-related tasks, such as sentiment analysis, text summarization, and question answering. By leveraging the techniques from statistical and neural machine translation, data scientists can enhance their natural language processing pipelines and develop more accurate and robust models.

In conclusion, statistical and neural machine translation are two pivotal approaches in the field of natural language processing. While statistical machine translation has a long-standing history and remains applicable in specific scenarios, neural machine translation has revolutionized the field with its ability to capture complex linguistic patterns. As data scientists and statisticians, understanding these approaches can empower you to tackle language-related challenges and leverage the power of machine translation in your work.

Language Generation Techniques

In the field of Natural Language Processing (NLP), language generation techniques play a vital role in transforming raw data into meaningful and coherent text. These techniques enable machines to generate human-like language, allowing us to communicate with computers in a more natural and efficient manner. This subchapter will delve into the various language generation techniques employed in NLP and their applications in data science and statistics.

One of the fundamental techniques used in language generation is template-based generation. This approach involves creating predefined templates with placeholders that can be filled with relevant data. By using templates, machines can generate text that follows a specific structure while incorporating specific information. Template-based generation is commonly employed in chatbots, automated customer support systems, and report generation.

Another widely used technique is rule-based generation. In this approach, language generation relies on a set of predefined rules or grammars. These rules dictate how different components of a sentence or text should be structured. By following these rules, machines can generate grammatically correct and coherent text. Rule-based generation is often used in text summarization, machine translation, and question answering systems.

Statistical approaches, such as n-gram models and language models, are also prominent in language generation. N-gram models analyze the frequency of word sequences in a given corpus to predict the next word or sequence of words. Language models, on the other hand, leverage statistical techniques to estimate the probability of a particular sequence of words occurring in a given context. These models enable machines to generate text that is not only grammatically correct but also contextually relevant.

Furthermore, recent advancements in deep learning have paved the way for neural network-based language generation techniques. Recurrent Neural Networks (RNNs) and its variants, such as Long Short-Term Memory (LSTM) and Gated Recurrent Unit (GRU), have demonstrated remarkable success in generating coherent and context-aware text. These models learn from large amounts of text data and capture the dependencies between words, leading to more natural and human-like language generation.

In conclusion, language generation techniques are essential in NLP for transforming raw data into meaningful and coherent text. Whether it's template-based generation, rule-based generation, statistical approaches, or neural network-based models, each technique has its own strengths and applications. Language generation techniques find extensive applications in the fields of data science and statistics, where generating reports, summarizing data, and answering questions require machines to generate human-like text. By leveraging these techniques, we can enhance our ability to communicate with machines and extract valuable insights from vast amounts of textual data.

Chapter 9: Text Summarization and Document Classification

Introduction to Text Summarization

In today's digital age, we are inundated with vast amounts of textual information from various sources such as news articles, research papers, and social media posts. With such an overflow of data, it becomes increasingly challenging for individuals to extract valuable insights efficiently. This is where text summarization comes into play.

Text summarization is a natural language processing technique that aims to condense lengthy documents into shorter, coherent summaries while preserving the essential information. It enables individuals to quickly grasp the main points and key details of a text without having to read the entire document. This subchapter will provide a comprehensive introduction to text summarization, covering its significance, techniques, and applications.

For data scientists and statisticians, text summarization offers a powerful tool to analyze and extract knowledge from large volumes of textual data. By automating the summarization process, data scientists can save time and resources while gaining valuable insights from diverse sources. Whether it is analyzing customer reviews, extracting key findings from research papers, or monitoring social media trends, text summarization can enhance the efficiency and accuracy of data analysis.

This subchapter will delve into various techniques used in text summarization, including extractive and abstractive approaches. Extractive summarization involves selecting and assembling important sentences or phrases from the original text, while abstractive summarization generates new sentences that capture the essence of the content. We will explore the strengths, limitations, and challenges associated with each technique, providing a holistic understanding of the field.

Furthermore, we will discuss the evaluation metrics used to assess the quality of text summarization systems. These metrics play a crucial role in comparing different approaches and determining their effectiveness. Additionally, we will highlight the recent advancements in text summarization, such as the integration of machine learning and deep learning techniques, which have significantly improved the quality and coherence of generated summaries.

Lastly, we will explore the practical applications of text summarization across various domains. From assisting journalists in quickly summarizing news articles to aiding researchers in reviewing vast volumes of scientific literature, text summarization has found its way into numerous industries. We will discuss real-world use cases and showcase how text summarization is revolutionizing data analysis and decision-making processes.

By the end of this subchapter, readers from all backgrounds will have a solid understanding of text summarization and its potential applications. Whether you are a data scientist, statistician, or simply interested in the field of natural language processing, this chapter will equip you with the knowledge to leverage text summarization techniques and unlock the power of textual data.

Extractive Summarization Techniques

In the journey from raw text to insightful knowledge, one crucial step is extracting the most important information from a given document or set of documents. This process, known as extractive summarization, involves identifying and condensing the key ideas and details while preserving the overall meaning. In this subchapter, we will delve into various extractive summarization techniques that play a vital role in the field of natural language processing (NLP).

Extractive summarization techniques aim to generate summaries by selecting and rearranging sentences from the source text, rather than generating new sentences. These techniques are particularly valuable for Data Science and Statistics professionals who deal with large volumes of textual data and need to quickly grasp the main points without reading the entire document.

One popular approach to extractive summarization is the use of graph-based algorithms. These algorithms construct a graph representation of the text, where nodes represent sentences, and edges denote the relationships between them. By leveraging graph-based algorithms, important sentences can be identified based on their centrality within the graph, such as degree centrality or PageRank scores. These sentences are then extracted to form a concise summary.

Another technique commonly employed in extractive summarization is the application of machine learning models. These models are trained on large datasets to learn patterns and features indicative of important sentences. By analyzing various linguistic features, such as word frequency, sentence position, and syntactic structure, these models can accurately predict which sentences should be included in the summary.

Additionally, advancements in deep learning have brought forth neural network-based models for extractive summarization. These models, such as the popular Transformer architecture, can effectively capture the contextual information and dependencies between sentences, enabling them to generate high-quality summaries. By training on massive amounts of data, neural network models can learn to summarize documents with remarkable accuracy and fluency.

It is crucial to note that while extractive summarization techniques provide efficient and informative summaries, they do not generate novel sentences or introduce new perspectives. The main advantage of extractive summarization lies in its ability to distill the essential information from a document, making it highly suitable for tasks like document clustering, information retrieval, or providing an overview of lengthy texts.

In conclusion, extractive summarization techniques serve as valuable tools in the field of natural language processing. By utilizing graph-based algorithms, machine learning models, and neural networks, these techniques enable Data Science and Statistics professionals to quickly extract key information from large volumes of text. Incorporating extractive summarization into NLP workflows can significantly enhance productivity and facilitate knowledge extraction from textual data.

Abstractive Summarization Techniques

In the rapidly evolving field of Natural Language Processing (NLP), one of the most fascinating and challenging tasks is abstractive summarization. As humans, we often have the ability to comprehend lengthy documents and distill the most important information into concise summaries. Abstractive summarization aims to replicate this cognitive process using computational models.

Abstractive summarization techniques utilize advanced algorithms and linguistic analysis to generate summaries that go beyond simply extracting sentences or phrases from the original text. These techniques aim to understand the context, extract key insights, and then generate a summary that captures the essence of the document.

One of the primary challenges in abstractive summarization is the generation of coherent and fluent summaries that maintain semantic accuracy. Unlike extractive summarization, which simply selects and concatenates sentences, abstractive techniques involve paraphrasing and rephrasing the original content to create a concise yet informative summary.

To achieve this, various approaches have been developed, including deep learning models such as Recurrent Neural Networks (RNNs) and Transformer-based architectures like BERT (Bidirectional Encoder Representations from Transformers). These models are trained on large datasets to learn patterns and generate summaries that are coherent, fluent, and faithful to the original text.

Another important aspect of abstractive summarization is the consideration of document-specific features such as named entities, sentiment, and discourse structure. These features help in identifying the most salient information and conveying it effectively in the summary.

Despite the advancements in abstractive summarization techniques, there are still several challenges that researchers are actively working on. These challenges include reducing redundancy in generated summaries, handling ambiguous references, and improving the overall fluency and coherence of the generated text.

Abstractive summarization has significant implications across various domains, including journalism, research, and data science. It enables quick information retrieval, aids in decision-making, and supports automated content generation.

For data scientists and statisticians, abstractive summarization can be a valuable tool in extracting insights from large volumes of textual data. By summarizing research papers, reports, or survey responses, they can efficiently analyze and make sense of the information, leading to more informed and data-driven decisions.

In conclusion, abstractive summarization techniques represent a significant advancement in NLP and have the potential to revolutionize the way we process and understand textual information. As these techniques continue to evolve, they will undoubtedly play a crucial role in enabling humans and machines to efficiently extract knowledge from text, empowering individuals across diverse domains.

Document Classification and Topic Modeling

In the era of big data, the amount of textual information available is growing exponentially. This wealth of text data holds valuable insights and knowledge that can greatly benefit various fields, including data science and statistics. However, the sheer volume of text makes it challenging for humans to manually analyze and categorize it effectively. This is where document classification and topic modeling come into play.

Document classification is the process of automatically assigning predefined categories or labels to documents based on their content. It is a fundamental task in natural language processing (NLP) that allows us to organize, search, and retrieve information from a large collection of documents efficiently. By leveraging machine learning algorithms, document classification algorithms can automatically learn patterns and features within the text and use them to predict the appropriate category for a new, unseen document.

Topic modeling, on the other hand, is a statistical technique that aims to discover underlying themes or topics within a large collection of documents. Unlike document classification, which assigns labels to individual documents, topic modeling focuses on uncovering the hidden structures and patterns that connect different documents based on their content. By identifying these topics, researchers can gain a deeper understanding of the key themes present in the data and explore relationships between different documents.

Both document classification and topic modeling have numerous practical applications across various domains. In data science, document classification can be used to automatically label customer reviews as positive or negative sentiment, classify news articles into different categories, or filter spam emails from legitimate ones. This allows data scientists to efficiently process and analyze large volumes of textual data, leading to more accurate insights and decision-making.

Similarly, topic modeling has wide-ranging applications in statistics. Researchers can use it to analyze large collections of scientific articles, identifying the main research themes or trends within a particular field. This can help statisticians and researchers stay up-to-date with the latest developments and make informed decisions about their own research directions. Topic modeling can also be applied to social media data to uncover trending topics or analyze public sentiment towards a particular issue.

In summary, document classification and topic modeling are powerful techniques that enable us to harness the value hidden within vast amounts of textual data. Their applications span across various fields, including data science and statistics, and offer valuable insights and knowledge. By automating the categorization and analysis of text data, these techniques empower researchers and practitioners to make more informed decisions and extract meaningful information from the vast sea of text.

Chapter 10: Natural Language Processing in Real-World Applications

Natural Language Processing in Voice Assistants

Natural Language Processing (NLP) has revolutionized the way we interact with technology, and one area where it has made significant strides is in voice assistants. These intelligent systems, such as Siri, Alexa, and Google Assistant, have become an integral part of our daily lives, helping us with tasks, answering questions, and even entertaining us. In this subchapter, we will explore the fascinating world of Natural Language Processing in voice assistants and how it has transformed the way we communicate with technology.

Voice assistants are built on NLP algorithms that enable them to understand and respond to human language. These algorithms analyze spoken or written input, break it down into smaller components, and extract meaning and context from it. By leveraging techniques such as speech recognition, natural language understanding, and dialogue management, voice assistants are able to comprehend user queries and generate appropriate responses.

One of the key challenges in NLP for voice assistants is speech recognition. Converting spoken words into text accurately is crucial for understanding user commands. Advanced machine learning models, such as deep neural networks, have greatly improved speech recognition accuracy, enabling voice assistants to understand a wide range of accents and languages.

Natural language understanding (NLU) is another critical component of voice assistants. NLU algorithms parse user queries, extract relevant information, and identify the intent behind the query. This allows voice assistants to provide appropriate and meaningful responses. NLU techniques include named entity recognition, part-of-speech tagging, and syntactic parsing.

Dialogue management is essential to maintain a coherent conversation between the user and the voice assistant. Systems need to remember previous interactions, handle interruptions, and generate appropriate responses based on context. Reinforcement learning and rule-based approaches are commonly used in dialogue management systems to ensure smooth and contextually relevant conversations.

Voice assistants are continuously improving through machine learning and the analysis of vast amounts of data. They learn from user interactions and adapt their responses over time, becoming more accurate and personalized. As a result, voice assistants have become indispensable tools for many individuals, aiding them in various tasks, from setting reminders and playing music to providing weather updates and answering general knowledge questions.

In conclusion, Natural Language Processing has played a pivotal role in the development of voice assistants. By leveraging techniques such as speech recognition, natural language understanding, and dialogue management, these intelligent systems have transformed the way we interact with technology. As advancements in NLP continue, voice assistants will become even more sophisticated, offering a personalized and seamless user experience. Whether you are a data scientist, statistician, or simply a technology enthusiast, understanding the intricacies of NLP in voice assistants is essential in comprehending the underlying technology that powers these ubiquitous digital companions.

Sentiment Analysis in Social Media

In today's digital age, social media platforms have become a hub for individuals to express their opinions and emotions freely. With billions of users active on platforms like Facebook, Twitter, Instagram, and more, these platforms have evolved into a treasure trove of valuable information. Sentiment analysis, a powerful technique in natural language processing (NLP), allows us to tap into this wealth of data and uncover the sentiments and emotions behind the vast amount of text generated on social media.

Sentiment analysis, also known as opinion mining, aims to extract subjective information from text and classify it into different sentiment categories such as positive, negative, or neutral. By analyzing social media content, we can gain valuable insights into customer opinions, public perception of brands, political sentiment, and much more.

For data scientists and statisticians, sentiment analysis offers a wide range of applications and opportunities for research. By harnessing the power of NLP and machine learning algorithms, they can build models that automatically detect sentiment with high accuracy. These models can be used to analyze social media data in real-time, helping companies make data-driven decisions, improve customer satisfaction, and monitor public sentiment towards their brand.

Sentiment analysis techniques can also be applied to gauge public opinion during elections, track public sentiment towards social issues, and even detect early signs of potential market trends. By analyzing social media conversations, data scientists can identify patterns, uncover hidden insights, and make predictions that were previously unattainable.

However, sentiment analysis in social media comes with its own set of challenges. Social media text is often informal, filled with slang, abbreviations, emojis, and grammatical errors, making it difficult for traditional NLP techniques to accurately analyze sentiment. Additionally, contextual understanding, sarcasm, and irony pose further challenges in accurately classifying sentiment.

This subchapter aims to provide an in-depth understanding of sentiment analysis in social media, addressing both the theoretical concepts and practical applications. It will cover various techniques used in sentiment analysis, including lexicon-based approaches, machine learning algorithms, and deep learning models. We will also explore the challenges and limitations of sentiment analysis in social media and discuss potential solutions to overcome them.

Whether you are a data scientist, statistician, or simply someone interested in understanding how sentiment analysis works in social media, this subchapter will equip you with the knowledge and tools to unlock the valuable insights hidden within the vast sea of social media data.

Text Mining in Healthcare

In recent years, the healthcare industry has been accumulating an unprecedented amount of data from various sources, such as electronic health records, clinical notes, research articles, and patient-generated content. However, extracting meaningful insights from this vast sea of unstructured text data has proven to be a daunting task. This is where text mining comes into play, revolutionizing the way healthcare professionals analyze and utilize this information.

Text mining, a subfield of natural language processing, involves the application of computational techniques to extract valuable knowledge from unstructured text. By employing advanced algorithms and statistical models, text mining enables healthcare providers to uncover patterns, trends, and relationships hidden within large volumes of textual data. This process not only facilitates evidence-based decision-making but also enables the development of innovative solutions to improve patient care and outcomes.

One of the primary applications of text mining in healthcare is clinical decision support. By analyzing a patient's medical history, symptoms, and laboratory results, text mining algorithms can help healthcare providers make accurate diagnoses and recommend appropriate treatment plans. Moreover, text mining can aid in the identification of adverse drug reactions, allowing for early intervention and prevention.

Another crucial area where text mining has made significant contributions is biomedical research. With the exponential growth of scientific literature, it is increasingly challenging for researchers to keep up with new discoveries. Text mining techniques automate the extraction and synthesis of relevant information, enabling scientists to identify potential drug targets, discover novel biomarkers, and gain insights into disease mechanisms.

In addition to clinical decision support and biomedical research, text mining also plays a vital role in healthcare surveillance and monitoring. By analyzing social media posts, online forums, and patient reviews, healthcare organizations can gain real-time insights into public sentiment, identify disease outbreaks, and track the effectiveness of public health campaigns.

However, text mining in healthcare is not without its challenges. Privacy concerns, data quality issues, and the need for domain-specific knowledge pose significant obstacles. Nonetheless, with advances in machine learning and natural language processing, these challenges are gradually being addressed, paving the way for even more sophisticated text mining applications.

In conclusion, text mining is a powerful tool that has the potential to transform healthcare by unlocking the hidden knowledge within vast amounts of unstructured text data. From clinical decision support to biomedical research and healthcare surveillance, text mining offers invaluable insights that can enhance patient care, improve outcomes, and drive innovation in the field. As the healthcare industry continues to embrace the digital revolution, text mining will undoubtedly play a pivotal role in shaping its future.

Natural Language Processing in Fraud Detection

Natural Language Processing (NLP) has emerged as a powerful tool in various fields, including fraud detection. In this subchapter, we will explore how NLP techniques can be applied to detect fraudulent activities and enhance the effectiveness of fraud detection systems.

Fraudulent activities have become increasingly sophisticated, making it challenging for traditional rule-based systems to keep up. This is where NLP comes in, offering a more intelligent and adaptive approach to fraud detection. By leveraging NLP, fraud detection systems can analyze large volumes of textual data, such as emails, customer reviews, social media posts, and financial reports, to identify patterns and anomalies indicative of fraudulent behavior.

One of the key applications of NLP in fraud detection is sentiment analysis. By analyzing the sentiment expressed in customer reviews or social media posts, organizations can identify potential fraudulent activities. For example, if a customer consistently posts negative reviews about a company's products but suddenly starts posting positive reviews, it could be a sign of fraudulent behavior, such as fake reviews to boost product ratings.

Another NLP technique, named entity recognition, can be used to extract important information from unstructured text data. By identifying entities such as names, addresses, and financial figures, fraud detection systems can quickly spot inconsistencies or discrepancies that may indicate fraudulent activity. For instance, if a customer's address changes frequently or if a company's financial reports contain suspicious numbers, it could be a red flag for fraud.

Moreover, NLP can also be used to analyze textual data for patterns that may indicate fraudulent behavior. By applying techniques such as topic modeling and clustering, fraud detection systems can identify groups of related documents or conversations that may be associated with fraudulent activities. For example, if a cluster of emails contains discussions about illegal transactions or fraudulent schemes, it can be a strong indication of fraudulent behavior.

In addition to these techniques, NLP can be used in conjunction with other data science and statistical methods to build more accurate fraud detection models. By combining textual data with structured data, such as transaction records or user profiles, organizations can create comprehensive fraud detection systems that leverage the power of NLP to uncover hidden fraudulent patterns and protect against financial losses.

In conclusion, NLP is a valuable tool for fraud detection in today's data-driven world. By analyzing textual data using techniques like sentiment analysis, named entity recognition, and pattern analysis, organizations can enhance their fraud detection systems and stay one step ahead of sophisticated fraudsters. Whether you are a data scientist or statistician, understanding the potential of NLP in fraud detection can greatly benefit your work and help safeguard against financial fraud.

Chapter 11: Challenges and Future Directions in Natural Language Processing

Challenges in Natural Language Processing

Natural Language Processing (NLP) is a field of study that focuses on enabling computers to understand and process human language. While NLP has made remarkable progress over the years, it still faces several challenges that researchers and practitioners strive to overcome. This subchapter explores some of the major challenges in NLP and the ongoing efforts to address them, catering to an audience of everyone, particularly those interested in data science and statistics.

One of the primary challenges in NLP is the inherent ambiguity of human language. Words and phrases can have multiple meanings depending on context, making it difficult for machines to accurately interpret them. Natural language understanding requires context-aware models that can disambiguate between different meanings and accurately represent the intended message. Researchers have developed various techniques, such as word embeddings and contextualized word representations, to tackle this challenge.

Another significant challenge is the lack of labeled training data. NLP models typically require large amounts of annotated data for training, but creating such datasets is time-consuming and expensive. Moreover, NLP tasks often require domain-specific annotations, which further limits the availability of labeled data. To address this challenge, researchers have explored techniques such as transfer learning and semi-supervised learning, which leverage pre-trained models and limited labeled data to achieve better performance.

The diversity and complexity of human language pose additional challenges. Languages vary in their structure, grammar, and syntax, making it difficult to build universal NLP models that can handle multiple languages effectively. Moreover, languages also evolve over time, introducing new words, phrases, and idioms that need to be incorporated into NLP systems. Researchers are working on developing language-agnostic models and techniques to handle language variations and adapt to evolving language patterns.

Ethical considerations also play a crucial role in NLP. Bias in training data can lead to biased models, resulting in unfair or discriminatory outcomes. For example, biased language models may generate offensive or harmful content. Researchers and practitioners are actively working on developing methods to detect and mitigate bias in NLP models, ensuring fairness and inclusivity.

In conclusion, NLP faces several challenges related to ambiguity, data availability, language diversity, and ethical considerations. Overcoming these challenges requires interdisciplinary efforts from linguists, statisticians, computer scientists, and domain experts. Despite the hurdles, progress in NLP has been significant, and the field continues to strive toward more accurate, context-aware, and unbiased natural language understanding. This subchapter provides a comprehensive overview of the challenges in NLP, serving as a valuable resource for anyone interested in data science, statistics, and the fascinating world of natural language processing.

Ethical Considerations in Natural Language Processing

In recent years, Natural Language Processing (NLP) has witnessed remarkable advancements, revolutionizing the way we interact with computers and enabling machines to understand and process human language. As NLP continues to evolve and permeate various aspects of our lives, it is crucial to address the ethical considerations that accompany this powerful technology. This subchapter explores the ethical implications and challenges associated with NLP, and aims to raise awareness among a diverse audience of data science and statistics enthusiasts.

One of the primary ethical concerns in NLP revolves around privacy and data protection. NLP systems often rely on vast amounts of user data, including personal information, to enhance their performance. However, the collection and utilization of such data raise significant privacy concerns. As individuals, we must be cognizant of the data we willingly provide and understand how it might be used, ensuring our consent is informed and protected. Additionally, developers and organizations must implement robust protocols to safeguard user data and ensure responsible data handling practices.

Another critical area in NLP ethics is bias and fairness. Language models are trained on extensive datasets, which can inadvertently encode biases present in the data. This bias can result in unfair and discriminatory outcomes, perpetuating societal inequalities. It is essential for NLP practitioners to actively identify and mitigate biases, promoting fairness and inclusivity in their models. This entails diverse and representative training data, as well as ongoing monitoring and evaluation to minimize unintended biases.

Transparency and explainability are additional ethical considerations in NLP. As NLP models become increasingly complex, they can be perceived as black boxes, making it challenging to understand their decision-making process. It is crucial to develop methods that provide interpretability, enabling users to comprehend how these models arrive at their conclusions. This transparency not only fosters trust but also allows for the identification and rectification of potential errors or biases.

Furthermore, the ethical implications of NLP extend to issues like misinformation, hate speech, and the potential for manipulation. NLP systems can inadvertently spread false information and amplify harmful content. Developers should prioritize the development of techniques to combat misinformation and hate speech, promoting responsible use of NLP technology.

In conclusion, as NLP continues to advance, it is imperative to address the ethical considerations associated with this powerful technology. By fostering privacy, fairness, transparency, and responsible use, we can maximize the benefits of NLP while minimizing the potential risks. As individuals, developers, and organizations, we must collectively strive towards ethical practices in NLP to ensure a positive impact on society.

Future Directions and Emerging Trends in Natural Language Processing

As the field of Natural Language Processing (NLP) continues to evolve, it is crucial to stay updated on the future directions and emerging trends that will shape the industry. In this subchapter, we will explore the exciting advancements and potential applications that lie ahead in NLP, addressing an audience of "everyone" and specifically catering to the niches of Data Science and Statistics.

One of the most significant future directions in NLP is the integration of deep learning techniques. Deep learning has already revolutionized various fields, and NLP is no exception. By leveraging neural networks and large-scale data, deep learning models have achieved remarkable results in tasks such as machine translation, sentiment analysis, and named entity recognition. Going forward, we can expect further advancements in deep learning architectures tailored specifically for NLP, leading to improved accuracy and efficiency in language-related tasks.

Another promising direction is the development of NLP models that can understand and generate human-like conversations. Conversational AI, powered by NLP, aims to create intelligent chatbots and virtual assistants capable of engaging in natural and contextually relevant conversations. This technology has already made significant strides, but future research will focus on enhancing the conversational abilities, empathy, and responsiveness of these systems, making them more indistinguishable from human interactions.

Furthermore, the integration of NLP with other emerging technologies such as knowledge graphs and graph databases holds immense potential. By combining the power of NLP with structured knowledge representation, we can create intelligent systems that can reason, infer, and answer complex questions in a more comprehensive and accurate manner. This integration will enable advancements in areas such as question answering, information retrieval, and knowledge discovery.

Additionally, there is a growing interest in multilingual and cross-lingual NLP. With the increasing globalization and interconnectedness of the world, the ability to process and understand multiple languages becomes crucial. Future research will focus on developing models that can handle multiple languages efficiently, enabling seamless communication and information retrieval across different linguistic boundaries.

Lastly, ethical considerations and bias in NLP will play a vital role in shaping its future. There is a growing awareness of the potential biases and ethical concerns surrounding NLP models, including issues of fairness, transparency, and privacy. Researchers and practitioners need to address these challenges and work towards developing more unbiased, transparent, and ethical NLP systems.

In conclusion, the future of NLP holds immense potential and exciting possibilities. From deep learning advancements to conversational AI, integration with other technologies, multilingual capabilities, and ethical considerations, the field is poised to transform the way we interact with and understand language. For those interested in Data Science and Statistics, staying updated on these future directions and emerging trends in NLP will be crucial for leveraging its power in various domains.

Chapter 12: Conclusion

Recap of Key Concepts

In this subchapter, we will provide a comprehensive recap of the key concepts covered in the book "From Text to Knowledge: A Comprehensive Guide to Natural Language Processing." Whether you are a data science professional or a statistics enthusiast, this recap will serve as a useful refresher on the fundamental concepts discussed throughout the book.

Natural Language Processing (NLP) is a branch of artificial intelligence that focuses on the interaction between computers and human language. It involves the application of computational techniques to analyze, understand, and generate human language in a way that is meaningful and useful.

One of the key concepts in NLP is text preprocessing. This involves cleaning and transforming raw text data into a format that can be effectively analyzed. Techniques such as tokenization, stemming, and stop-word removal are commonly used to preprocess text data and improve the quality of the analysis.

Another important concept is sentiment analysis, which aims to determine the sentiment or emotional tone of a piece of text. Sentiment analysis techniques can be used to analyze customer reviews, social media data, and other forms of text data to gain insights into public opinion and attitudes.

Topic modeling is another significant concept in NLP. It involves discovering the underlying themes or topics within a collection of documents. Techniques such as Latent Dirichlet Allocation (LDA) and Non-negative Matrix Factorization (NMF) are commonly used for topic modeling and can help in organizing and summarizing large volumes of text data.

Named Entity Recognition (NER) is a technique used to identify and classify named entities in text, such as names of people, organizations, locations, and dates. NER is an essential component in various NLP applications, including information retrieval, question answering systems, and machine translation.

Additionally, the book covers the concept of text classification, which involves assigning predefined categories or labels to text documents based on their content. Text classification algorithms, such as Naive Bayes, Support Vector Machines (SVM), and deep learning models like Convolutional Neural Networks (CNN) and Recurrent Neural Networks (RNN), are commonly used in this context.

Finally, the book delves into the concept of word embeddings, which represent words or phrases as dense numerical vectors in a high-dimensional space. Word embeddings capture semantic relationships between words and have revolutionized various NLP tasks, including language modeling, machine translation, and sentiment analysis.

By revisiting these key concepts, you will solidify your understanding of the fundamental principles of NLP and gain insights into how these techniques can be applied to real-world problems in the domains of data science and statistics.

Importance of Natural Language Processing in the Data Science and Statistics Field

Natural Language Processing (NLP) has emerged as a crucial tool in the field of data science and statistics, revolutionizing the way we extract, analyze, and interpret information from vast amounts of textual data. As more and more data is generated every day, NLP offers powerful techniques to process, understand, and make sense of this unstructured data, unlocking valuable insights and knowledge.

One of the primary reasons for the importance of NLP in the data science and statistics field is the sheer volume of text-based data available today. From social media posts and customer reviews to scientific articles and legal documents, a vast amount of valuable information is embedded in text. However, manually analyzing and extracting insights from this data is a daunting task. NLP techniques, such as text classification, sentiment analysis, and topic modeling, allow data scientists and statisticians to automate the process, making it faster, more efficient, and scalable.

Furthermore, NLP plays a crucial role in data preprocessing. Text data often contains noise, irrelevant information, or inconsistencies that can hinder analysis. Through techniques like text cleaning, tokenization, and stemming, NLP helps to transform raw text into a clean and structured format, enabling accurate analysis and modeling. By effectively preprocessing text data, NLP ensures the quality and reliability of statistical analyses.

Another significant application of NLP in data science and statistics is in information retrieval. NLP-powered search engines, recommendation systems, and question-answering systems have become indispensable tools for researchers, analysts, and decision-makers. By understanding the context, intent, and semantics of user queries, NLP algorithms can provide highly relevant and accurate search results, recommendations, and answers, enhancing the efficiency of data-driven decision-making processes.

Moreover, NLP techniques enable the extraction of structured information from unstructured text, a process known as information extraction. Named Entity Recognition (NER), relationship extraction, and event extraction are some NLP techniques used to identify and extract valuable information from text, such as names, dates, organizations, and relationships. This extracted information can then be used for statistical analysis, trend identification, and predictive modeling, providing valuable insights for various applications, including market research, fraud detection, and healthcare analytics.

In conclusion, NLP plays a pivotal role in the field of data science and statistics by enabling efficient processing, analysis, and interpretation of vast amounts of text-based data. With its ability to preprocess, retrieve, and extract valuable information from unstructured text, NLP empowers data scientists and statisticians to uncover hidden patterns, trends, and insights, ultimately leading to more accurate and informed decision-making in a wide range of industries and domains.

Final Thoughts and Further Resources

Congratulations! You have reached the end of this comprehensive guide to natural language processing (NLP). We hope that this book has provided you with a solid foundation and understanding of the various concepts and techniques involved in NLP. Now, it's time to reflect on what you have learned and explore further resources to expand your knowledge in this exciting field.

Throughout this book, we have covered a wide range of topics, from the basics of text processing and linguistic analysis to more advanced techniques such as machine learning and deep learning for NLP. We have discussed the challenges and complexities of working with natural language data, and provided practical examples and code snippets to help you implement these techniques in your own projects.

As you delve deeper into the world of NLP, you will discover that there is always something new to learn and explore. To continue your journey, we recommend exploring the following resources:

1. Online Communities and Forums: Engage with the vibrant NLP community by joining online forums and communities. Websites like Stack Overflow, Reddit, and Kaggle have dedicated sections for NLP where you can ask questions, share ideas, and learn from others' experiences.

2. Books and Research Papers: NLP is a rapidly evolving field, and staying up-to-date with the latest research is crucial. Look for books and research papers authored by experts in the field. Some recommended books include "Speech and Language Processing" by Daniel Jurafsky and James H. Martin, and "Natural Language

Processing with Python" by Steven Bird, Ewan Klein, and Edward Loper.

3. Online Courses and Tutorials: Several online platforms offer comprehensive courses and tutorials on NLP. Websites like Coursera, Udemy, and edX provide courses taught by industry professionals and leading researchers. These courses often include hands-on exercises and projects to strengthen your practical skills.

4. NLP Toolkits and Libraries: Familiarize yourself with popular NLP toolkits and libraries such as NLTK, SpaCy, and TensorFlow. These libraries provide a wide range of functionalities and pre-trained models that can be used to accelerate your NLP projects.

Remember, the key to mastering NLP lies in practice. Explore real-world datasets, participate in Kaggle competitions, and work on personal projects to gain hands-on experience. NLP is a fundamental component of data science and statistics, and mastering it will open doors to exciting career opportunities.

We hope that this book has inspired you to dive deeper into the world of NLP and has equipped you with the necessary knowledge and tools to tackle real-world challenges. Good luck on your NLP journey, and may you continue to unlock the power of text and knowledge!

www.ingramcontent.com/pod-product-compliance
Lightning Source LLC
Chambersburg PA
CBHW070000180726
48002CB00018B/1009